# Migration, Remittances and Household Socio-Economic Wellbeing: The Case of Ethiopian Labour Migrants to the Republic of South Africa and the Middle East

**Asnake Kefale and Zerihun Mohammed**
FSS Monograph No. 14

ፎረም ፎር ሶሻል ስተዲስ
**FORUM FOR SOCIAL STUDIES (FSS)**

ISBN: 978-99944-50-66-4


Forum for Social Studies (FSS)

P.O. Box 25864 code 1000

Addis Ababa, Ethiopia

Email: fss@ethionet.et

Web: www.fssethiopia.org.et

This Monograph has been published with the financial support of the he International Organization for Migration (IOM) through its *African, Caribbean and Pacific- European Union (ACP-EU) Migration Action*. The contents of the Monograph are the sole responsibilities of the authors and can under no circumstances be regarded as reflecting the position of the IOM, ACP-EU or the FSS.

# Contents

## Acknowledgement

In the course of this study, we received generous support from various organizations and individuals. We would like to extend our gratitude to all these institutions, government offices, and experts. We are particularly grateful to the International Migration Organization (IOM) for its financial support through its *African, Caribbean and Pacific- European Union* (ACP-EU) *Migration Action*. We are also grateful to our colleagues, W/ro Melat Gezahegn and Ato Abera Woldekidan, for their valuable contribution in data collection and analysis. We would also like thank to our informants in the regions and Addis Ababa who candidly answered our questions during the fieldwork.

## About FSS

The Forum for Social Studies (FSS) is a non-government, non-profit organization engaged in promoting informed public debate through policy oriented research. FSS' work is guided by the conviction that enhancing the interface between the public and policy makers on key social and economic issues can promote a transparent, participatory and all-inclusive policy-making and implementation process.

Since its establishment in 1998, FSS has been engaged in policy research on a wide array of development issues, and has disseminated its findings to policy makers and the wider public. It has organized a series of policy dialogues (workshops, seminars, panel discussions, etc.) around the themes of poverty; gender; higher education; inter-generational transfer of knowledge; good governance and democracy in Africa; culture and development; and climate change, environmental management and sustainable development in Ethiopia. As part of its research activity, FSS has published large number of books and monographs on a wide range of development and policy issues, including, poverty and poverty reduction, natural resource management, decentralization, the quality of higher education, culture and development, and environment and climate change.

This monograph on *Migration, Remittances and Household Socio-Economic Wellbeing: The Case of Ethiopian Labour Migrants to the Republic of South Africa and the Middle East* is a continuation of that tradition, and is intended to promote dialogue and constructive debate on the issue of labour migration and remittances among different stakeholders

## List of Tables

## List of Figures

# 1    INTRODUCTION

## 1.1    The Problem

In recent years, remittance flows from abroad to Ethiopia have become significant in terms of total volume as well as the attention they received from policy makers. In this respect, the National Bank of Ethiopia (NBE) reported that the amount of remittance flowing to Ethiopia has increased from 3.04 billion USD in 2013/14 to 3.99 billion USD in 2015/16 (NBE, 2016). Members of the Ethiopian diaspora and Ethiopian migrant workers remit a large sum of money to their families. The remittance money that comes to the country greatly contributes to the wellbeing of migrant families and to the national economy as well. Indeed, remittances have become important sources of foreign exchange for Ethiopia. For example, in recent years remittances have outperformed the export sector in bringing foreign exchange to the country (NBE, 2016).

However, it is strongly believed that substantial amount of remittances still comes to the country through informal channels. The choice of channel for remittance is often determined by multitude of factors, the major of which is the migrants' preference to transfer remittance money to their host countries. Undocumented migrants cannot use financial institutions including banks and money transfer agencies. For instance, a recent study conducted by the Forum for Social Studies(2015) showed that a large number of Ethiopian migrants in the Republic of South Africa use various informal channels of transferring remittance money as those migrants do not have the necessary legal documents that offer them access to formal bank services in the host country. On the Ethiopian side, there are a number of factors that undermine the use of formal remittance transfer channels. Firstly, and most importantly, the variance in the exchange rate of hard currencies between the formal and the 'informal' market is usually high. As a result, people prefer the informal channel of transferring remittances, which will be discussed in detail later on, as it usually gives more money in the Ethiopian currency (Birr) than the formal/bank transfer. Secondly, limitations in accessibility of financial services encourage people to use the informal channel.

Regarding the purpose the remittance money is used, studies indicated that the remittances received by families and relatives of migrants are primarily used for household consumption, followed by asset building, such as for house construction, purchasing vehicles to be used to engage in transport services business, and setting up small businesses (Sander and Maimbo, 2005; De Hass, 2007).

The way recipient families use remittance money is also found to have some negative consequences. Conflict over the control and use of the money among family members and the tendency to continually depend on remittances are some of the negative consequences of remittance.

In spite of the growing literature on migration from Ethiopia (ILO, 2015; Asnake and Zerihun, 2015; Fernandez, 2009), there is limited understanding about the impact of remittance flows on household wellbeing and the channels that migrant workers and members of the diaspora use to remit money to their families, relatives and friends. As discussed in the next sections, remittances include financial and non-financial or in-kind transfers. In this study, we limit ourselves to financial transfers, which could be used either for consumption or for asset building.

Based on these premises, this research project examined the various channels through which Ethiopian labour migrates in the Republic of South Africa and the Middle East countries send remittance to their families; and how remittance money is utilised at household levels. By doing so, the study provides insights that will be useful to the effort to strengthen the use of formal channels of transferring remittance money. The research also provides insights that would be beneficial in the effort of designing strategies that would encourage families not only to use remittance money efficiently, but also to engage in income generating activities.

The focus on Ethiopian labour migrants to the Republic of South Africa and the oil rich Middle Eastern countries was because of two major reasons. First, unlike most of the migrants to Europe and North America, the majority of the migrants to these two destinations are economic migrants with the ultimate aim of making as much money as possible in the host countries and eventually returning to Ethiopia to lead a decent life. Hence, remittances, either be for family support or personal savings, play an important role in one's migration-decision.

Secondly, the current research is built upon two earlier research reports. The first is a monograph entitled *Ethiopian Labour migration to the Gulf and South Africa* (2015), which culminated from FSS's research on labour migration in which it investigated the genesis, routes, processes, impacts and policy implications of labour migration from Ethiopia to those destinations. Remittance and its roles as cause and effect of migration was one of the issues seen in the research. The second one is a report from an important study that was conducted by the International Organization for Migration (IOM), in collaboration with the Foreign Ministry of the Federal Democratic Republic of Ethiopia (FDRE), in which they examined factors that undermine formal remittance transfers to Ethiopia and provided policy recommendations that could enhance the formal financial sector (Isaacs, 2017).

## 1.2    Objectives of the Study

The overall objective of the study is to examine the various channels Ethiopian labour migrants in the Republic of South Africa and the Middle East use to send remittance to their families and its contribution to the wellbeing of the families. By doing so, the study aims to identify the various challenges and opportunities associated with the formal and informal money transfer mechanisms.

The specific objectives of the research were to:

a. Identify the various formal and informal channels of remittance transfers used by Ethiopian labour migrants in the Republic of South Africa and the Middle East;

b.  Examine the challenges and opportunities of using formal and informal remittance transfer channels by Ethiopian labour migrants;

c.  Examine the patterns of remittance use by remittance-receiving families;

d.  Analyse the positive and negative impacts of remittances on households' socio-economic wellbeing; and

e.  Draw recommendations that help to improve the efficiency and effectiveness of formal remittance transfer channels and the use of remittance in more economically productive areas.

## 1.3  Study Sites

The data and information for the study were collected from ten systematically selected *woredas*,[1] two from each of four regional states (Tigray, Amhara, Oromia and Southern Nations Nationalities and Peoples Region –SNNPR) and Addis Ababa City Administration, which are the major regional states in terms of population and geographical size. The *woredas* (see Table 1) were selected based on the prevalence of migration of people to the Republic of South Africa and the Middle East, the flow of remittances from those destinations to the migrants' places of origin, and socio-economic impacts (Asnake and Zerihun, 2015; FSS, 2017).

---

[1]*Woreda* is an Amharic term for district.

Table 1: Study sites in each region/city administration

| No. | Region | Zone | Woreda/Sub-city |
|-----|--------|------|-----------------|
| 1. | Tigray | Eastern Zone | Adigrat |
| | | Southern Zone | Mekelle |
| 2. | Amhara | South Wollo | Kombolcha |
| | | North Wollo | Wereilu |
| 3. | Oromia | South Arsi | Shashemene |
| | | South Arsi | Kofele |
| 4. | SNNP | Hadiya | Hosa'ena |
| | | Halaba Special *woreda* | Halaba |
| 5. | Addis Ababa | - | Addis Ketema |
| | | - | Kirkos |

## 1.4    Respondents and methods of data collection

A research team was deployed to the study *woredas* to collect primary data for a period of one month (between January 15 and March 30, 2018). Different methods of data collection were applied to gather the necessary primary and secondary data (quantitative) and information (qualitative) from different sources. The major primary data collection methods were survey, key informant interviews, and focus group discussions. In addition, the research team also collected secondary data from *woreda* Administration Offices, Labour and Social Affairs Offices, the National Bank of Ethiopia, the World Bank and the Central Statistical Agency (CSA).

### Key informant interviews (KIIS)

Key informant interviews (KIIs) were extensively used to collect qualitative data from the study sites. The key informants were selected based, among others, on their migration history, receipt of remittances, and position in relevant government and private organizations. Returnee migrants from South Africa and the Middle East and families with a family member(s) that currently migrated to the one or both of those destinations were specifically targeted for interview. The KIIs with those returnee migrants were meant to understand migration trends, channels of remittance transfer and use of the remittance money in the households. Moreover, managers and officers of local branches of government and private banks were interviewed to understand the magnitude of formal transfers in the study sights (localities). Heads and experts of *Woreda* and zonal Micro and Small Enterprises, Social and Labour Affairs Offices, Technical and Vocational Education and Training (TVET) and Microfinance Institutions were also interviewed in order to gain insights about the challenges that households face in the use of remittance money for asset building and other non-consumption/productive expenditures.

## Focus Group Discussions

Focus group discussions (FGDs) were employed to get collective views of the returnee migrants and their families. Two types of FDGs were conducted in each *woreda*: one type with returnee migrants and another type with family members of migrants. Accordingly, a total of 20 FGDs (one for the returnee migrants and one for families of migrants in each *woreda*) were conducted. Each focus group was composed of six to nine men and women purposively selected from the communities based on their information, knowledge and personal experience on the subject of migration and remittance in their communities.

## Secondary data

Secondary data and information used for this study were obtained from *woreda* Administration offices and Labour and Social Affairs Offices, the National Bank of Ethiopia, the World Bank and the Central Statistical Agency (CSA). The data from the *Woreda* Social and Labour Affairs offices were used to understand the dynamics of labour migration in each *woreda* and to select sample population for the survey discussed below. The data from the National Bank of Ethiopia was used to analyse the pattern and trends of remittance

money coming to the country in recent years. Similarly, the CSA data was used to know the size of the population of each region and *woreda*, which was important in the selection of the sample field areas.

## Survey

The survey was used to collect quantitative data from the study *woredas*. Two separate surveys were undertaken for the study: one for the returnee migrants and the other for the families of migrants.

The survey questionnaires to the returnee migrants were targeted to people who returned home after migrating to the two destinations. It was decided to approach returnee migrants as it is be impractical to include migrants who at the time of the survey were working in the Republic of South Africa and the Middle East. The length of their stay (a minimum of two years) as labour migrants in their destinations was used as the sole criterion of the selection of the returnee population. Using the list of returnees obtained from the Labour and Social Affairs Offices in the study *woredas*, a sample of 25 respondents was drawn from each *woreda,* making a total sample of 250 returnee migrants.

The survey addressed to returnee migrants was used to acquire pertinent data on issues, such as:

- How and why they migrated,
- Whether they were sending remittance to their families or not,
- If yes, how much and how often,
- What means or channels they were using, and
- Challenges and opportunities associated with the use of the formal or the informal means of remittance transfer.

The second survey was designed for household heads of families that, at the time of the survey, have migrant family members in the Republic of South Africa and the Middle East. This survey was mainly intended to understand the socio-economic impacts of remittances on the wellbeing of the recipient households. These respondents were identified by local officials at the *Kebele*[2] level. Accordingly, 20 households were selected from each *woreda*, making a total of 200 respondents.

## 1.5    Significance of the Study

The researchers strongly believe that the study has practical significance. By using qualitative and quantitative data, it aims to identify key trends in the transfer of remittance to Ethiopia and the socio-economic impacts of remittance at household level. By doing so, it contributes insights that would be helpful in the effort to strengthen formal transfer of remittances to the country and the use of remittance money for asset building.

## 1.6    Limitations of the Study

This study is limited to migrants to the Republic of South Africa and the Middle East. These two destinations attract a large number of Ethiopian economic migrants. As prior studies such as Asnake and Zerihun (2015), Demissie (2017), and Gebre, Maharaj and Pillay (2011) showed economic push and pull factors are the primary forces influencing decisions to migrate to these destinations. Thus, we believed, focusing on these two regions has a potential to disclose about migrant workers' choice of remittance transfer channels and the utilization of the funds by their families at home. However, the study did not cover Ethiopians and people of Ethiopian descent who live permanently in other parts of the world, including North America, Europe and Oceania. These migrants, often referred as Ethiopian Diaspora, also remit funds to the country either to support their families or to engage in investment projects. We were, however, unable to include these groups because of time and resource constraints. In spite of this, the findings of this study provide insights about the choice of remittance transfer channels, the way remittance money is used by recipient families and the socio-economic impacts of remittances on the recipient families.

---

[2]*Kebele* is the lower level of administrative unit in urban areas under *woreda*, or district.

# 2 REMITTANCE FLOWS AND SOCIO-ECONOMIC IMPACTS: REVIEW OF LITERATURE

## 2.1 Global Trends

Remittances refer to financial and in-kind transfers from migrant individuals back to their countries of origin. Adams Jr. (2011:809) defines remittances simply as "the money and goods that are transmitted to households by migrant workers working outside of their origin communities, either in urban areas or abroad" (Adams Jr. 2011:809). For others, the international dimension is amplified. Alemayehu, Kibrom and Meleket (2011) note that "transactions that are initiated by individuals living or working outside their country of birth or origin and related to their migration" could be conceptualized as remittances. Kapur (2003:2) adopts a similar conception of remittances as "financial resource flows arising from the cross-border movement of nationals of a country". He, however, identifies two types of remittance transfers. The first is 'unrequited transfers' which refer to "money sent by migrants to family and friends on which there are no claims by the sender". The second type refers to transfers which are not meant for consumption and include money meant for debt settlement, savings and investment (Kapur, 2003:2). As noted in the introductory part, this study deals with all financial transfers, including money sent for consumption, debt settlement, savings and investment.

In recent years, remittances from migrants have gained greater attention due to their contribution to the economies of developing countries in terms of foreign exchange receipts, investment, and supporting the livelihoods of migrants' families. Globally, flow of remittances has been increasing steadily as the number of people who live outside their country of origin increased as a result of growing international migration (see United Nations, 2017). In the last few decades, a large number of people migrated to destinations far and wide for various reasons, including violence and political repression at the places of origin and search for better economic wellbeing elsewhere. This has also resulted in increased remittances, as individuals send money back home; whether to support families left behind, payback loans to people that initially facilitated their migration, or to simply invest in their home countries. According to a United Nations migration report, the number of international migrants has climbed from 173 million in 2000, to 220 million in 2010 and 258 million in 2017, which shows an average yearly growth of above two per cent (United Nations, 2017). The size of remittances to developing countries worldwide meanwhile was estimated to be USD 444 billion by 2017, which is up from USD 429 billion in 2016 (World Bank, 2017). This is a tremendous increase, considering the fact that remittances worldwide were estimated to be less than USD 2 billion in 1970, and just about USD 70 billion by 1995 (Taylor, 1999:68).

The global share and distribution of remittances is uneven as some regions perform better than others. Data for the period from 2010 to 2016, for instance, shows that East Asia and the Pacific as well as South Asia received the largest remittance inflows, followed by Latin America and the Caribbean. While the Middle East and North Africa performed lower than the above regions, Sub-Saharan Africa received the smallest flows in the entire period (World Bank, 2017). Taking the 2015 inflows as an example, East Asia and the Pacific received USD 127.3 billion followed by South Asia with USD 117.6 billion. Middle East and North Africa and sub-Saharan Africa (SSA), on the other hand, received 51.1 and USD 35.1 billion, respectively for the same period (World Bank, 2017). Globally, the top remittance-recipient countries for the year 2016 were India, China, Philippines, Mexico and Pakistan in that particular order. From sub-Saharan Africa, Nigeria ranked 6th in the top ten list (World Bank, 2017).

SSA still receives lesser amount of remittances in comparison to other regions. As of 2017, out of the 258 million international migrants worldwide, 36 million, making up 16.6 per cent of the total, were Africans (United Nations, 2017:9). However, the region receives a small fraction of global remittance flows. In 2016 for instance, remittance flows to the region were estimated just USD 33

billion out of the global flows to developing countries, which were estimated USD 429.3 billion. Sub-Saharan Africa's share from the global transfer stood at a mere 7.7 per cent (World Bank, 2017). There is little improvement over a long-time span, as SSA's share of global remittance flows was just 5 per cent of the total in 2003, which is small compared to 16per cent share garnered by the Middle East and North Africa in the same period (Sander and Maimbo, 2005:56).

Due to a host of factors including high cost of transfer and weak financial systems and services, a large volume of money is informally remitted to sub-Saharan Africa (Sander and Maimbo, 2005:55). Indeed, the cost of sending remittances to sub-Saharan Africa is the highest, with an average of 9.7 per cent for sending USD 200 in 2016, which was above the global and developing country average. The average cost of sending remittances was 5.5 per cent for South Asia, 5.9per cent for Latin America and the Caribbean, and 7.5per cent for the Middle East and North Africa (World Bank, 2017). Even if it is difficult to have a realistic estimate of the size of remittances transferred informally, the share of informal remittances is higher in Africa than in other parts of the world; and that is because of 'weak or absent financial systems, high rates of intraregional migration, and frequent physical transport of remittance monies' (Sander and Maimbo, 2005:56).

Whichever channel they are remitted through, remittances to Africa have macroeconomic, micro-economic, and communal impacts (Mohapatra and Ratham, 2011; Sander and Maimbo, 2005). In terms of macroeconomic impact, remittances are an important source of financial inflows to the African continent, serving as an important source of foreign exchange, contributing to the national balance of payments, and representing a substantial share of GDP (Nisah, Christian and Bichaka, 2018). In terms of microeconomics, remittances are a welfare mechanism that support consumption, provide insurance and 'alleviates liquidity constraints' (Sander and Maimbo 2005:62). Overall, remittances in Africa are primarily used for consumption and investment in human capital like education, health, and better nutrition (Nisah, Christian and

Bichaka, 2018:723; Sander and Maimbo 2005:63). In addition, smaller portion of remittances are used for investment in land, livestock, housing and business development (Sander and Maimbo 2005). While there has always been a debate on the impact of remittances on economic growth and development in the recipient countries, growing evidence and academic consensus tilts to the argument that the positive impacts of remittances are far greater than their disadvantages. These positive impacts range from macroeconomic benefits in terms of foreign exchange gains and easing balance of payments deficits to potential microeconomic impacts on poverty, welfare, food security, investment capital and improved consumptions, as well as impacts on health, education and infrastructure, among others (Mohapatra and Ratham, 2011; Nisah, Christian and Bichaka, 2018).

Taylor (1999), in a pioneering study about the development potential of remittances from the perspective of the New Economics of Labour Migration (NELM), underscores that impacts of remittances on development could be seen from two levels. First, "migration decisions are part of family strategies to raise income, obtain funds to invest in new activities, and insure against income and production risks; and second, remittances, "set in motion a development dynamic by loosening production and investment constraints faced by households in poor developing country environments" (Taylor, 1999:64). Additionally, Taylor argues, "market linkages transmit the impacts of migration from migrant to non-migrant households in the sending economy" (Taylor, 1999:80). This shows that if migrant remittances contribute positively to incomes, they might have a multiplier effect on incomes, employment, and production in migrant sending economies (Taylor, 1999:69). Since households and firms are linked together through markets, "expenditure linkages transmit the impacts of remittances from the remittance receiving households to other households and production firms in the economy" (Taylor, 1999:69)

In addition, remittances showed more stability and reliability than other forms of capital inflows did to developing countries. In an often-quoted work that also reignited interest on remittance studies, Ratha (2003) makes a strong case for the argument that remittances are a relatively more reliable and stable, least volatile, source of much needed foreign exchange for developing countries than other forms of capital flows. Even after major recent international financial crises of 2008 and 2011, remittances remained remarkably stable in comparison to foreign direct investment (FDI) and official development assistance (ODA) (Yang, 2011; UNCTAD, 2012).

The preceding short discussion showed the growing consensus about the positive roles of remittances to the migrant-sending countries. Specifically, there is a widely shared consensus among scholars about the contribution of international migration and remittances to reducing poverty in the developing world (Adams and Page, 2005; Ratha, 2013).

## 2.2    Trends and Patterns of Remittance Flows in Ethiopia since the 1990s

Recently, remittance flows to Ethiopia have become significant in terms of total volume as well as the attention garnered from policy makers. Although there are some variations in the reporting of the volume of remittance transferred to Ethiopia by different institutions, all evidence suggests that there has been a substantial increase in the volume of remittances in the past two decades. The World Bank (2011), for instance, reports that remittance flows to Ethiopia increased substantially from USD27 million in 1995 to USD 53 million in 2000 and reached 387 million by 2010, averaging 1.3 per cent of GDP in 2009 (World Bank, 2011). In 2012, the National Bank of Ethiopia (NBE) reported that remittances to Ethiopia reached USD 1.74 billion, surpassing export revenue for the same year which stood at USD 1.6 billion (Ghosal, 2015:177). This amount, however, seems to have increased significantly, as NBE reports that 'net private individual transfers' were  USD 3.04 billion, USD 3.7 billion, and USD 3.99 billion for the years 2013/14, 2014/15 and 2015/16 (NEB, 2015/16). That amounted to 7.4 per cent, 7.6 per cent and 8.3per cent of GDP for the same year (NEB, 2016/17).

The major source regions for remittance more or less overlap with the major destinations of migrants: North America, The Gulf Cooperation Council (GCC) countries, and Europe. In 2004, the United States of America, Israel, and Germany were the largest sources countries for remittances that amounted to USD 46 million, 25 million and 10 million, respectively (Alemayehu, Kibrom and Meleket, 2011:5, IMF, 2005). Ghosal (2015:182), quoting a 2009 United Nations report, writes that North America is the principal source of remittances to Ethiopia with a 41 per cent share of total inflows, followed by Europe and Asia with 29 and 24 per cent of inflows, respectively. Alemayehu and Irving (2011:115) write that the major sources of remittance to Ethiopia were the United States of America and the Gulf Cooperation Council (GCC) countries, especially United Arab Emirates (UAE), Bahrain, Saudi Arabia and Kuwait.

**Figure 1**: Remittance to Ethiopia 1990 – 2016 (USD in Millions)

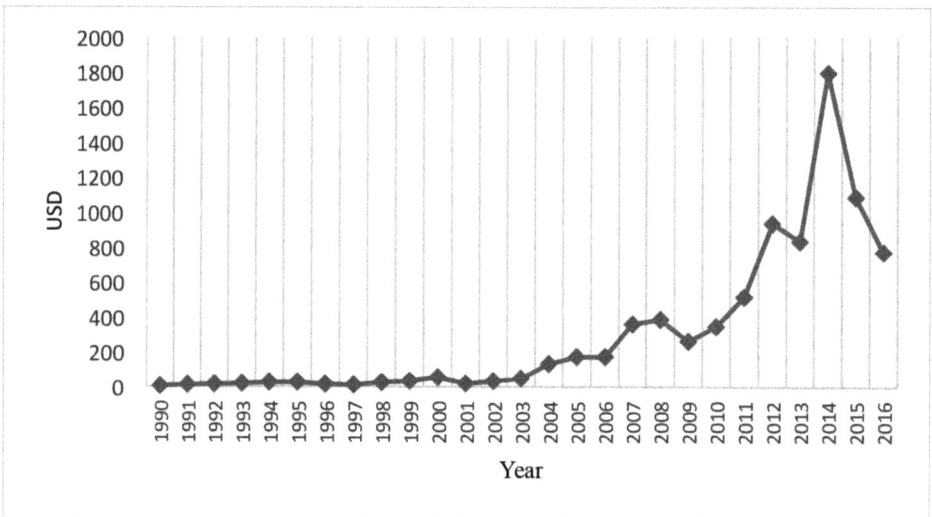

*Source:* World Bank, 2016

The data in Figure 2 show that remittance flows were increasing only slightly, from 5.21 million USD in 1990 to USD 27.35 million in 1995 and to USD 46.45 million in 2003. While this period represents slow increments, the figure jumped to USD 133.74 million in 2004, rose to USD 386.69 million by 2008 and then sharply climbed to an all-time high of USD 1.79 billion by 2014, after which it registered a decline. The data in Figure 2 below, which contains 'individual private transfers' as reported by the NBE, show substantially higher figures.

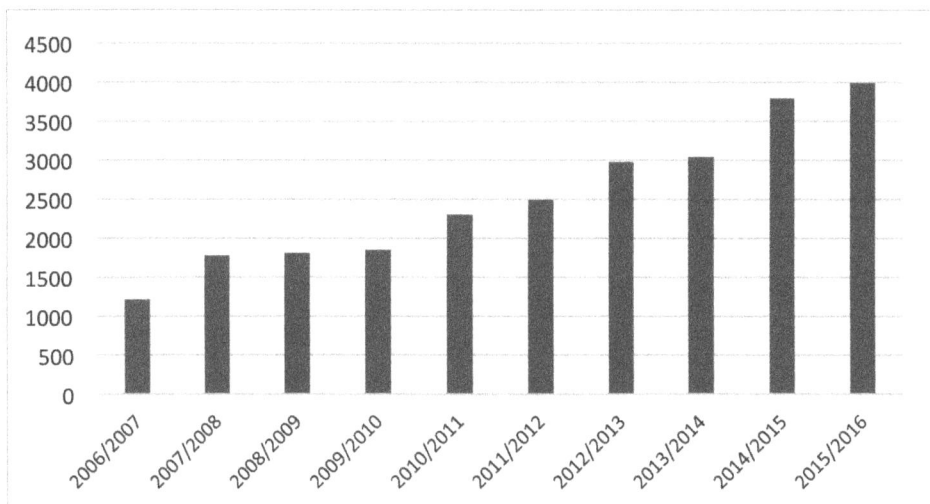

**Figure 2:** Individual private transfers to Ethiopia (2006/2007 – 2015/16) (USD in Millions (*Source:* NBE Reports various years)

These NBE figures for 'individual private transfers' show that remittances have surpassed USD 1 billion since the 2006/07 fiscal year, reaching close to four billion by the 2015/16 fiscal year. The category 'individual private transfers', as employed by the NBE, incorporates three sub-categories: 'cash', 'in kind' and 'underground private transfers'; and that explains why the figures here are substantially higher than other estimates. While 'cash' refers to official transfers, 'underground private transfers' refers to estimates of informal individual transfers. For instance, in 2009/10, the volume of overall private individual transfers was USD 1,847.3 million (see Figure 2 above). Out of this, 'cash' (the official transfer) was USD 790.3 million while 'underground private transfers' (informal flows) accounted for USD 960.3 million. The difference, USD 96.7 million, was 'in kind' transfers.

Three basic observations can help to understand the importance of remittances to the Ethiopian economy. The first is the remittance-to-GDP ratio, which indicates how much remittances are contributing to the overall economy. Both the World Bank and NBE data show that this ratio has been rising steadily. While NBE data (above) shows that remittances accounted, on average, for 7 to 8 per cent of GDP, Isaacs (2017) estimated that it accounted for five per cent of GDP, while contributing to one quarter of foreign exchange earnings. The second one is comparing remittances to export earnings. Over the past two decades, remittances have not only caught up with export earnings, but also have consistently outperformed them in recent years. Thirdly, remittances can also be compared to other capital flows to the country, like FDI and ODA. In this respect, remittances have performed beyond expectations. As indicated earlier, remittance in Ethiopia has outperformed FDI in 2010, even by World Bank figures, as remittance was USD 387 million compared to 100 million in FDI. ODA figures, however, were higher than remittances for the same year, as it stood at 3.3 billion USD. As this study showed, remittances have positive impacts on household welfare as well.

## 2.3    Remittance Transfer Channels

From the above discussion and figures, it is possible to deduce that the majority of remittance inflows to Ethiopia are informal, which is why they are not captured by World Bank official figures. Isaacs (2017:6) argues that while the government of Ethiopia has managed to increase the formal flows of remittances in recent years, the informal channels are still the main means for Ethiopians to send money home, estimating this flow to be as much as 78 per cent of total remittance inflows 'in some corridors'. This raises three main questions: 1) why do people choose to use informal channels? 2) What mechanisms do these informal channels involve? 3) What efforts have been undertaken by the government to encourage the use of formal channels?

Several factors have the potential to explain why migrants choose informal channels to send money home instead of the formal mechanisms. Russell (1992, cited in Alemayehu, Kibrom and Meleket, 2011:4), argues, "individuals' choice between formal and informal channels for sending money back home depends on the socio-economic characteristics of their household members, level and type of economic activity in the host countries, exchange rate and sending charge differentials and relative efficiency of the formal sector relative to the informal sector". Isaacs (2017:6), on the other hand, argues that, "Lack of access to services in the sending and receiving markets, high direct and indirect costs associated with formal channels, irregular migration, the existence of parallel market exchange rates, and regulatory barriers for undocumented migrants contribute to the high level of informal transfers". Many of these factors explain why remittance flows to Ethiopia are predominantly informal.

First, exchange rate differentials are an important factor. Exchange rates in the black markets offer a higher value in local currency than if recipients were to collect their remittances directly from banks. The difference is high enough to incentivize migrants to choose to send cash directly to their relatives back home so that they can fetch a higher value in the informal channel. In Mid-May, 2018, for instance, while one USD is exchanged for about 27 ETH Birr in formal transfer channels, this margin can go as high as 35 birr in parallel informal channels (black market). The exchange rate difference is estimated anywhere between 5 per cent and 15per cent and significantly influences the decisions of remittance senders (Isaacs, 2017:77). One reason informal remittance service providers outperform the formal sector is their ability to offer services at a lower cost and charge 'foreign exchange commission at a better (black market) rate' (Alemayehu and Irving, 2011:125–126).

Secondly, socio-economic conditions and locations of recipient families are important determinants. If recipient family members are too impoverished to have access to financial services, senders prefer using informal channels to formal ones. The same logic applies when recipient household members live in remote localities, where financial services like banks and other remittance service providers are missing or where the available ones are not accessible. In this regard, a significant progress has been achieved in terms of expansion of banking services in Ethiopia, from 389 branches in 2005 to 2,693 branches in 2015 (Isaacs, 2017:64). However, compared to the geographic and population size, access to remittance payout locations and financial services in general remain a main problem in rural areas, with the number of poor rural households without access to formal financial services reaching 85 per cent (Isaacs, 2017:64–65). A related factor here can be recipients' lack of acceptable identification cards (IDs). For instance, private banks had a limited range of acceptable ID requirements for providing remittance services, 'which could impede the ability of the poorest recipients, particularly those dwelling in rural areas, to collect remittances from them (Alemayehu and Irving, 2011:125–126).

Third, the legal status of the migrants and the level and type of economic activity they are engaged in determines their choice. If an Ethiopian migrant is undocumented in the host country, that precludes access to formal financial services and is, thus, forced to use informal channels. This is also the case if the migrant is involved in irregular and/or informal work for which s/he cannot access formal financial services. These two interrelated factors explain the case of Ethiopian labour migrants in the Republic of South Africa and the Middle East , estimated 60 per cent of the total migrant population, are undocumented economic migrants and, thus, not likely to have access to formal remittance services(Isaacs,2017:60).

The regulatory and business environment makes it difficult for an efficient formal sector to flourish and thus leads to the dominance of the informal remittance transfer mechanisms. Alemayehu and Irving (2011) identify various obstacles in the regulatory and business environments that hinder entry into and functioning of formal remittance transfer service providers in Ethiopia. First, "the process of obtaining a license from NBE to provide remittance transfer services can be time consuming and lengthy" and can run up to two years. Another problem relates to "access to financial infrastructure" including inability to "undertake remittance outflow" as a result of regulations and lack of access to financial institutions and capital. Thirdly, "the lack of a modern national payment system and, in particular, the lack of a real-time gross

settlement (RTGS)" meant "there is no effective common clearing and settlement system linking all the banks". Thus, clearing remittance transfers from one bank to another is time consuming. Weak telecom infrastructure, especially in rural areas, is another problem for remittance-transfer-service providers as it hinders fast money transfers. Finally, competition from the informal providers was seen as a major obstacle (Alemayehu and Irving, 2011:124)

High costs of transfer, inefficiency, and/or unavailability of formal remittance transfer channels are important factors that explain the thrive of the informal remittance transfer channels. As discussed in the previous sub-section, the costs of remittance transfer are higher for Sub-Sahara Africa, with an average of 9.7 per cent for sending USD 200 in 2016, which was above the global and developing country average (World Bank, 2017). The service charge was 7.2 per cent for Ethiopia in the third quarter of 2016, which was, in fact, lower than both the global average and many Sun-Saharan African countries (Isaacs, 2017:74). However, this was still not an insignificant amount as it involved losing USD 7 for every 100 dollars transferred and, thus, can be a disincentive to using formal channels (Isaacs, 2017:74).

A related barrier is the time it takes to transfer to pay out locations in Ethiopia, although this is partially a matter of perception. As a World Bank survey data shows, 64 per cent of providers transfer in less than one hour (Isaacs, 2017:86). However, challenges of transferring to remote branch locations still remain as a result of poor telecom infrastructure with unavailable or intermittent internet connectivity, which creates unpredictability and delays than the World Bank survey suggests(Isaacs, 2017:86).

Finally, lack of awareness about the limited available formal money transfer services and lack of trust can influence the choice of individuals. Additionally, the limited presence of service providers, like postal services, credit unions, microfinance institutions, and telecom service providers is an obstacle as they have the right infrastructure to become viable alternatives (Alemayehu and Irving, 2011:118).

The methods for informal transfer of remittances include the following, among others. The first and most obvious pattern is sending cash through returning family members and friends. The other is the use of *Hawala*[3] services, which are seen as cost-effective and more reliable. Isaacs (2017:13) defines informal remittances as "remittances that do not pass through officially-regulated businesses at both the send and receive ends of a transaction" and involve informal methods of transfer like "hand carrying foreign currency, giving foreign currency to someone travelling to Ethiopia, using an unregulated money transfer operator (often known as *hawala*), or sending physical goods" (Isaacs, 2017:13). This is not a uniquely Ethiopian phenomenon as a substantial flow of remittances pass through informal/underground channels throughout the world 'outside the purview of government supervision and regulation' (Kapur, 2003:12). These methods go centuries back, especially in Asia, and include systems like "*hawala* and *hundi* (South Asia), *feich'ien* ([the People's Republic of] China), *phoekuan* (Thailand), *Hui* (Vietnam), *casa de cambio* (South America)", primarily flourishing in conditions where there are 'economic controls, political instability, and low levels of financial development' (Kapur, 2003:12).

---

[3]The term *hawala* has become an Amharic word to refer to formal transfer of money through formal banking and postal services (Ethiopian Languages Research Centre, 2001). However, in this study the term *hawala* is used in its original meaning to refer to the semi-organized informal money transfer system.

# 3    ANALYSIS AND FINDINGS

## 3.1    Description of the Sample Population

As explained above,  two types of surveys have been conducted: one for
returnee migrants and one for the migrant families. This section describes these
two sample populations in brief.

### 3.1.1    Characteristics of returnee migrants

Of the 250 sample population, 72.4 per cent of them were females, while the
remaining 27.6 per cent were males. The sample contained more number of
women than men mainly because of the fact that the majority of the Ethiopian
migrants travelling to the Middle East are women that are willing to work as
domestic workers (see Asnake and Zerihun, 2015; Bina, 2010). Age wise, 73.6
per cent of the sample population were between 21 and 32 years of age. Only
3.6per cent of them were under 20 years of age; and 2.0per cent were above 45
years of age. This indicates that a good proportion of the migrants travelling to
the Middle East and the Republic of South Africa are young people that are in
their most productive age.

In terms of education, 53.6 per cent of the sample population attended high
school, while about 35per cent of them were between grades 5 and 8. Six per
cent of the sample population had either a degree or diploma before they
migrated to their respective destinations. About three-quarter of the sample
population were not married at the time of their migration, while 23.2per cent of
them were married. Two per cent of them were divorced before they migrated
out.

Regarding employment status, 43.2 per cent of the sample population were
unemployed when they migrated; 32.8 per cent of them were students at
different grades. Only 11.2 per cent of the sample population had jobs as petty
traders, farmers and employees at different government and private
organizations. This indicates that unemployment was one of the main push

factors for many of the migrants at all levels. Considering the migrants' motives for migrating, the need to support one's families (54.0 per cent) and aspiration to lead a better life for oneself (41.2 per cent) were the major reasons for migrating. In terms of means of migration, about 60 per cent of them used private employment agencies, while the 33.6 per cent of them migrated to the destination countries without legal permits. Sixty per cent of the 50 migrants from the Tigray region and 50 per cent of the 50 migrants from the SNNP region travelled by crossing borders without fulfilling the necessary documentation, accounting for 38.0 per cent and 35.4per cent of the total migrants who crossed borders illegally, respectively. The geographical proximity of the Tigray region to the border and the long-established tradition of out migration in the region are the major factors, which explain the high rate of irregular migration from the region. Of the 50 sample population from the Tigray region, 44 per cent travelled to the Republic of South Africa without obtaining visa.

In terms of the amount of the money the migrants spent to migrate out, 54.4 per cent reported their spending were in the range of 1,000 to 10,000 birr. The highest cost of migration was reported to be 100,000 birr which was used for migration to the Republic of South Africa by air using a tourist visa. The fact that large percentage of the migrants spent relatively less money is because most of them claim to migrate through the overseas employment agencies, in which the prospective migrant worker is expected to cover only the cost of documentation and medical costs. Table 2 summarizes the major features of the sample migrant/returnee population.

**Table 2:** Characteristics of migrant/returnee sample population

| No. | Variable | Response sets | Frequency | Percentage |
|---|---|---|---|---|
| 1. | Sex | Male | 69 | 27.6 |
| | | Female | 181 | 72.4 |
| 2. | Age | <20 | 9 | 3.6 |
| | | 21–26 | 87 | 34.8 |
| | | 27–32 | 97 | 38.8 |
| | | 33–38 | 36 | 14.4 |
| | | 39–44 | 16 | 6.4 |
| | | 45–50 | 5 | 2.0 |
| 3. | Education | Grades 1–4 | 13 | 5.2 |
| | | Grades 5–8 | 88 | 35.2 |
| | | Grades 9–12 | 134 | 53.6 |
| | | Degree or diploma | 15 | 6.0 |
| 4. | Marital status before migrating | Unmarried | 187 | 74.8 |
| | | Married | 58 | 23.2 |
| | | Divorced | 5 | 2.0 |
| 5. | Employment status and type of job before migrating | Unemployed | 108 | 43.2 |
| | | Student | 82 | 32.8 |
| | | Small business owner/trader | 32 | 12.8 |
| | | Private organization employee | 13 | 5.2 |
| | | Government employee | 8 | 3.2 |
| | | Farmer | 7 | 2.8 |
| 6. | Country of destination | Saudi Arabia | 143 | 57.2 |
| | | Lebanon | 31 | 12.4 |
| | | Dubai | 27 | 10.8 |
| | | Republic of South Africa | 27 | 10.8 |
| | | Kuwait | 16 | 6.4 |
| | | Qatar | 4 | 1.6 |
| | | Libya | 2 | 0.8 |
| 7. | Major reason(s) for migration | To support my family financially | 135 | 54.0 |
| | | To better my own life | 103 | 41.2 |

| | | | |
|---|---|---|---|
| | Just for the sake of going abroad | 6 | 2.4 |
| | Pressure from family and friends | 4 | 1.6 |
| | Political reasons | 1 | 0.4 |
| | Pressure from brokers and agencies | 1 | 0.4 |
| 8. Means of migration | Legally via agencies | 149 | 59.6 |
| | On the pretext of pilgrimage (Hajj and Umra) | 12 | 4.8 |
| | Crossing borders illegally | 84 | 33.6 |
| | On the pretext of visit | 5 | 2.0 |
| 9. Total expense incurred for the migration (in *Birr*) | 1,000–10,000 | 136 | 54.4 |
| | 10,001–20,000 | 51 | 20.4 |
| | 20,001–30,000 | 26 | 10.4 |
| | 30,001–40,000 | 9 | 3.6 |
| | 40,001–50000 | 7 | 2.8 |
| | 50,001–60,000 | 5 | 2.0 |
| | 60,001–70,000 | 4 | 1.6 |
| | 70,001–80,000 | 2 | 0.8 |
| | 80,001–90,000 | 6 | 2.4 |
| | 90,001–100,000 | 4 | 1.6 |

### 3.1.2 Characteristics of Migrants' Families

The total size of the sample population of the migrants' families was 200 (20 household heads from each *woreda*). They were randomly selected among families with a member who had migrated to the Republic of South Africa or to the Middle East as labour migrants.

The data presented in Table 3 show that among the 200 sample household heads of the migrants' families, 53 per cent of them were women, while the remaining 47 per cent were men. Daughters and sisters constitute the largest portion of the migrants from the families (48.0 per cent and 23.5 per cent, respectively), followed by brothers (9.5 per cent), sons (8.5 per cent) and wives (4.5 per cent).[4]

In terms of destination, 55.5 per cent of the sampled household heads indicated that members of their families had migrated to Saudi Arabia in different forms; 12.5 per cent said to the Republic of South Africa, 11 per cent said to Dubai, and 8.5 per cent said to Lebanon. Concurrent with the responses from the sample population of returnee migrants, 44 per cent of the sampled household heads of migrants' families attested that the migrants were unemployed; 42.5 per cent of the household heads said that the migrants had been students before they migrated to their destination countries. Among the respondent household heads, 58.1 per cent said that they believed the migrants decided to migrate to improve their families live; while 34.5per cent of the respondents said, "the migrants moved because of the need to improve their own lives" (Table 3).

Regarding the occupation of the migrants' families, 34.0per cent of the respondents were farmers, followed by petty trade and small businesses (19.5%). There are families who relied on the support from other family members (8.0 per cent), safety net (5.0 per cent), income from casual work (5.0per cent), income received from renting houses/rooms (5.0 per cent) and pensions (3.5 per cent). Large percentage of the sampled families of migrants (42.0 per cent) indicated that their families survive with a monthly income of less than Birr 1,000; while 27.5 per cent earn up to Birr 2,000/month. Only 13.5 per cent of the respondents have monthly income between Birr 4,000 and 6,000. This indicates that, considering the current high living costs, the majority of the families lead a very modest living standard.

Just like the returnees, the majority of the household heads of the migrants' families said that the migration of their family members incurred financial cost

---

[4] In the survey, the researchers attempted to single out the share of the remittance money from families' total annual income. However, the information regarding families' annual income was found to be less reliable as people have poor or no recording of their incomes. As a result, it was not possible to calculate the exact ratio of remittance money out of household's total annual income.

from 1,000 to 10,000 birr. This cost was to cover the expenses for passport, medical certificate, police clearance and payment to the overseas employment agencies.

**Table 3:** Characteristics of migrant families sample population

| No. | Variable | Response sets | Frequency | Percentage |
|---|---|---|---|---|
| 1 | Sex of the respondent | Male | 94 | 47.0 |
| | | Female | 106 | 53.0 |
| 2 | Family economic sources | Farming | 68 | 34.0 |
| | | Petty trade and small business | 39 | 19.5 |
| | | Employed in private and governmental organizations | 36 | 18.0 |
| | | Support from family members | 16 | 8.0 |
| | | Safety net | 10 | 5.0 |
| | | Casual works | 10 | 5.0 |
| | | Income from house/room renting | 10 | 5.0 |
| | | Pension | 7 | 3.5 |
| | | Craft and related trades works | 4 | 2.0 |
| 3 | Estimated monthly income | <1000 | 84 | 42.0 |
| | | 1001–2000 | 55 | 27.5 |
| | | 2001–3000 | 24 | 12.0 |
| | | 3001–4000 | 10 | 5.0 |
| | | 4001–5000 | 12 | 6.0 |
| | | 5001–6000 | 8 | 4.0 |
| | | >6001 | 7 | 3.5 |
| 4 | Relationship with the migrant | Daughter | 96 | 48.0 |
| | | Sister | 47 | 23.5 |
| | | Brother | 19 | 9.5 |
| | | Son | 17 | 8.5 |
| | | Wife | 9 | 4.5 |
| | | Niece and nephew | 6 | 5.0 |
| | | Husband | 4 | 2.0 |
| | | Father | 1 | 0.5 |
| | | Cousin | 1 | 0.5 |
| 5 | Country of Migration | Saudi Arabia | 111 | 55.5 |
| | | The Republic of South Africa | 25 | 12.5 |
| | | Dubai | 22 | 11.0 |

| | | | | |
|---|---|---|---|---|
| | | Lebanon | 17 | 8.5 |
| | | Kuwait | 15 | 7.5 |
| | | Sudan | 5 | 2.5 |
| | | Oman | 4 | 2.0 |
| | | Qatar | 1 | 0.5 |
| 6 | Job of the migrant family member before migration | Unemployed | 88 | 44.0 |
| | | Student | 85 | 42.5 |
| | | Small business owner | 12 | 6.0 |
| | | Private employee | 10 | 5.0 |
| | | Farmer | 3 | 1.5 |
| | | Government employee | 2 | 1.0 |
| 7 | Family members 'reasons for migration | Support one's own family financially | 150 | 58.10 |
| | | Seeking a better life for oneself | 89 | 34.5 |
| | | Pressure from family and friends | 10 | 3.9 |
| | | Political reasons | 1 | 0.4 |
| | | Pressure from brokers and agencies | 4 | 1.6 |
| | | For the sake of going abroad | 1 | 0.4 |
| | | Escape unwanted marriage | 3 | 1.2 |
| 8. | Total amount incurred for the migration (in *Birr*) | 1,000–10,000 | 105 | 52.5 |
| | | 10,001–20,000 | 43 | 22.6 |
| | | 20,001–30,000 | 13 | 6.8 |
| | | 30,001–40,000 | 5 | 2.6 |
| | | 40001–50000 | 9 | 4.7 |
| | | 50,001–60,000 | 3 | 1.6 |
| | | 60,001–70,000 | 3 | 1.6 |
| | | 70,001–80,000 | 7 | 3.7 |
| | | 80,001–90,000 | 9 | 4.7 |
| | | 90,001–100,000 | 3 | 1.6 |

## 3.2 Remittance Flow from the Republic of South Africa and the Middle East to Ethiopia

As noted earlier, remittance flows from Ethiopian migrant workers in the Middle East and the Republic of South Africa to the migrants' families in Ethiopia. In fact, remittance has more importance for these migrants as their primary motive to migrate is the quest for employment opportunity that enables them to change their and their family's lives for the better. Consequently, the majority of migrants start to send money back home from the earliest days they manage to make money in their countries of destination. As shown in Table 4, the vast majority (that is close to 96 per cent) of the returnee migrants expressed their sending money to their families at different points in time and forms, and 91.5 per cent of the household heads of the migrants' families witnessed their receiving remittance through different channels. Only 4.4 per cent of the migrants said they did not remit money to the families back home, 3.2 per cent of them because of not having enough money to send to the families and 1.2 per cent because they were unwilling to remit to their families.

**Table 4:** Responses of returnee migrants on sending/receiving remittance

| Category | Question | Yes | | No | | Total | |
|---|---|---|---|---|---|---|---|
| | | Freq. | % | Freq. | % | Freq. | % |
| Migrant/Returnees | Were you sending money back home when you were abroad? | 239 | 95.6 | 11 | 4.4 | 250 | 100 |
| Migrant families | Do you receive remittance from your family member living abroad? | 183 | 91.5 | 17 | 8.5 | 200 | 100 |

Regarding how and when they send remittance, 34.3 per cent of the returnee migrants and 36.0 per cent their families claimed they received remittances regularly, while 36.3 per cent of the returnee migrants and 31.5per cent of the families said they send and receive, respectively, remittance when there is a need from the family. The major reasons that urge families to ask for remittances were illness, paying children's school fees, purchasing seed and fertilizer, and building/maintaining houses. The average amount of money sent on demand ranges between birr 5,001 and 10,000.

**Figure 3:** Percentage of time when migrants send remittances to their families back home

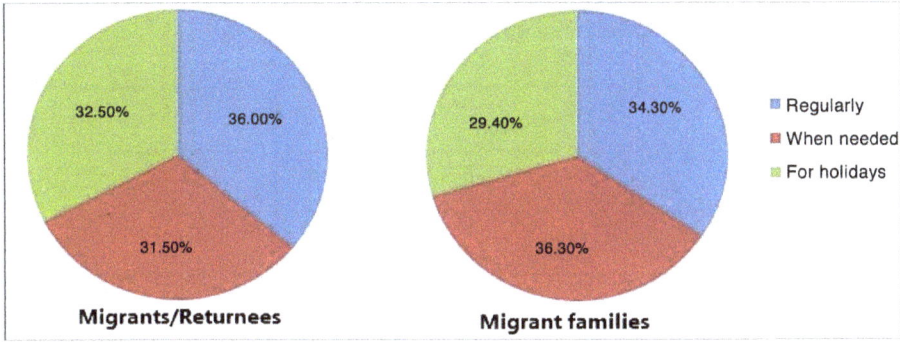

When we look how regular the remittance is sent, out of the 86 returnee migrant respondents who indicated their sending remittance to their families regularly, 55.8 per cent send money every three months, while only 3.5 per cent of them remittance in a year (Figure 4). In terms of amount, 37.2 per cent of them send on average between Birr 1,000 and 5,000 (which is equivalent to about USD 37.00–185.00), while 32.6 per cent of them send money in the range of Birr 5,001 to 10,000 (which is USD 185.00–370.00) regularly.

**Figure 4:** Frequency of regular remittances sent by returnee migrants

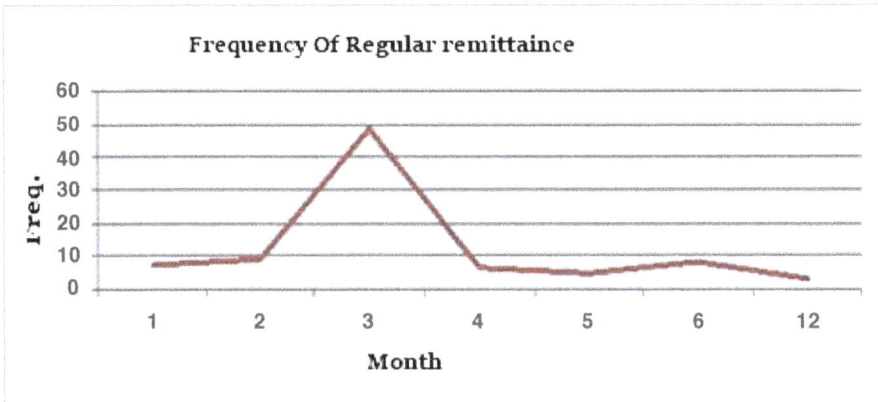

**Figure 5:** Amount of regular remittance sent by returnee migrants

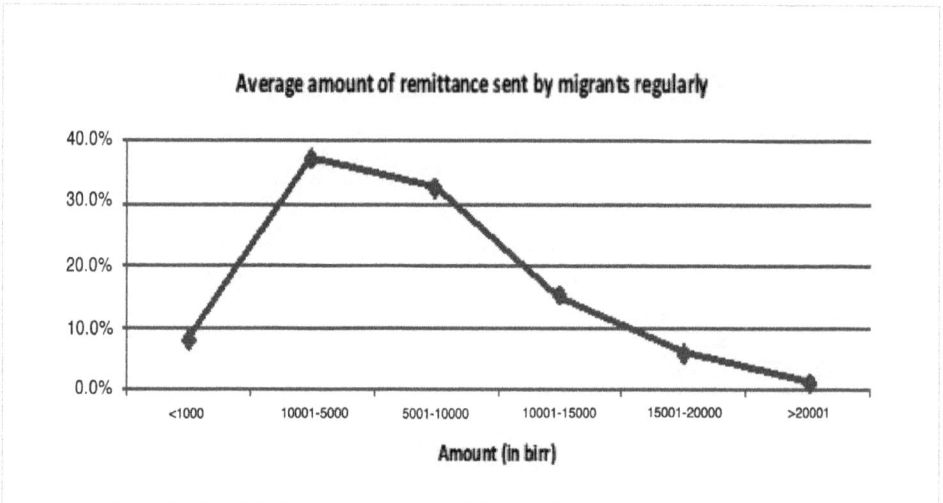

Average amount of remittance sent by migrants regularly

Returnee migrants used to remit sizeable amount of money to their families for holidays. Of the total amount of remittance sent for holidays, 18.9 per cent was sent for Easter and Christmas each, 16.2 per cent was sent for *Eid Al adha* and *Eid Al fatar* each, 14.9 per cent was sent for New Year, 9.5 per cent for *Mesqel* (the Founding of the True Cross), and 5.4 per cent for Epiphany. The smallest amount sent for such events was Birr 1,000 (USD 27.50) while the largest was Birr 10,000 (USD 27.00).

## 3.3    Channels of Remittance Transfer

Remittance is sent using the formal and informal channels, both of which have their own advantages and drawbacks for the senders and receivers. Returnee migrants were asked which transfer channels they most often use. Half of them replied that banks and money transfer institutions (such as Western Union and Money Gram) were their preferred channels, while the remaining half of them said they were using individuals travelling to the country and informal *hawala* as their channels for sending remittance to their families (see Table 5).

**Table 5:** Most used/preferred channels of remittance

| Channels of Remittance Transfer | Returnee Migrants | | Migrant Families | |
|---|---|---|---|---|
| | Frequency | Percentage | Frequency | Percentage |
| Bank/Money transfer institutions | 125 | 50.0 | 144 | 72.0 |
| Individuals/*Hawala* | 125 | 50.0 | 56 | 28.0 |
| Total | 250 | 100.0 | 200 | 100.0 |

As can be seen in Table 5 above, the majority of the migrant families (72 per cent) indicated that they receive remittance through banks and money transfer institutions, while only 28 per cent assert they receive through informal channels. This variation is, as will be explained in detail in the next sub-section, due to the fact that also the informal channels (*hawala*) use the bank systems to deliver the money to the recipients. Once the *hawala* operator receives the money in the host country, he/she gives order to his/her agent in Ethiopia to effect the payment in *birr* with full details (name, mobile phone number and addresses) of the recipient. The agent communicates with the recipient with the telephone number given and asks if the recipient has a bank account and if not, the convenient bank and branch to deposit the money in his/her name. With this, the recipient ultimately receives the money through the bank system and, thus, erroneously assumes that he/she got the money through the formal channel.

### The formal remittance transfer channel

The formal transfer systems, as explained in section two, are those that are operated by formal financial institutions and supervised by government agencies and governed by law determining the conditions and rules of their creation, operation and closure. In this regard, the financial regulating bodies of the sending and receiving counties have full control over and supervision of the transaction. In Ethiopia, all government-owned and private banks, plus other money transfer institutions, are engaged in transferring remittance in the formal channel. In this regard, probably because of its early operation in the area of international money transfer, Western Union has become quite popular institution in the country[5].

According to the informants in different government and private banks, the use of the formal method is a straightforward system in which the migrants transfer their money to the designated recipients through certain banks. The recipient is expected to present a valid identification card and a security number of the transfer given to him by the sender. The bank/money transfer institutions may ask questions such as the identity of the sender and the amount of money sent to ensure the authenticity of the person claiming the money. The recipient should not necessarily have account in the bank from which he/she collects the remittance money although many banks we interviewed encourage their remittance-receiving clients to open a saving account[6].

One of the major advantages of the formal system is its reliability. The senders have legal documents for the money they send to their families and can easily track it. Consequently, the chance of losing one's money in the process is almost nil. The other advantage of the formal transfer system, unlike the informal ones, is that it is legal and does not break any laws of the country. Besides the benefits the individuals concerned are getting, it contributes to the national economy by bringing foreign currency to the country.[7]

In spite of its straightforward nature and contribution to the national economy, however, formal transfer system has some serious limitations that hinder remittance-sending migrants from using it. According to informants, the first drawback of the system is the fact that migrants who want to send money using

---

[5] In one focus group discussion in Shashemene, South Arsi, a group of people were using the terms Western Union to refer all forms of money transfer institutions.

[6] Interview with Mr. Gebregzher Tekelemariam, Commercial Bank of Ethiopia, Adigrat Branch Manager (March 28, 2018); Mehari, Wegagen Bank, Mekelle Branch Manager, (March 23, 2018); Mr. Bisrat Asfaw, NIB international Bank, Kirkos Branch Manager (Feb, 12, 2018).

[7] Interview with Mr. Abebaw Bekele, Senior Branch Controller at Commercial Bank of Ethiopia, Kalu Branch, Kombolcha (March, 19, 2018); Mrs. Mahder Ambaye, Enat Bank, Mekelle Branch Manager (March 12, 2018). Girma Tafete, Commercial Bank of Ethiopia Worellu Branch Customer Service Manager (March 10, 2018).

the system need to present valid documents such as passport and residence permits, to the sending financial transfer institute. As a good deal of the Ethiopian migrants in the Republic of South Africa and the Middle East are illegal migrants, they are unable to present such documents and process their transfer. Even those labour migrants who went to the Middle East through the employment agencies, their passports are often taken away by their employers as part of the *kefala* (sponsorship) system[8] which ties the migrant worker with the employer.

Regarding the major challenges to use the formal system while they were labour migrants in the Republic of South Africa or the Middle East, two fifth of the respondents (40.4 per cent) identified lack of legal access to formal financial institutions as the primary factor that deterred them from using the system (Table 6). The migrants noted that they tried to solve the problem by using various methods. The first and widely common 'solution' was sending through other migrants who have such valid documents. The second common 'solution' used by migrants who used to work for individual households was to request their employers to send the money to their families on their behalf[9].

The returnee migrants identified that the second disadvantage of using the formal channel is the lower exchange rate it provides compared to the informal market, which gives usually higher rates. In Ethiopia, foreign currency exchange rates are centrally controlled and uniform in all banks; and always lag behind the informal market exchange rate for all major foreign currencies. However, there are times when the difference between the formal and informal

---

[8]Interview with Mrs. Emebet Jemal, Head of the Halaba Special Woreda Administration; Mrs. Tigist Gebrehiwot, Acting Head of Halaba Special *Woreda* Women and Children Affairs (Feb. 23, 2018).

[9]Interview with Ms. Isha Mohammed, returnee migrant from Saudi Arabia, Shashemene (February 21, 2018). Interview with Sofiya Hasen, Kofele (February 24, 2018).

exchange rates is significant on overall amount of money families receive in Birr[10].

**Table 6:** Major challenges of the returnee migrants to use formal remittance channels

| Challenges to use formal remittance transfer system | Response | |
|---|---|---|
| | **Freq.** | **%** |
| I am unable to use bank services because of my legal status | 101 | 40.4 |
| Exchange rate is lower in the banks | 67 | 26.8 |
| The process of sending money in the banks is complex | 37 | 14.0 |
| They are not accessible to my parents/relatives | 19 | 7.0 |
| They charge a lot of money | 14 | 5.0 |
| The money does not reach quickly | 12 | 4.0 |
| Total | 250 | 100.00 |

The third most important factor indicated by 14 per cent of the returnee migrants as a challenge of the formal system is the 'complexity' of money transfer process of the banking institutions. This is presumably the case as a large number of Ethiopian migrants are less educated and have little knowledge of how the formal transfer system works – a challenge that is exacerbated by their lack of knowledge of local languages (Arabic in the case of Middle East and English in the case of the Republic of South Africa). The respondents indicated that they were often troubled by their inability to speak the languages and to express themselves or what they need in the money transfer institutions. Although the institutions often show willingness to support, informants argued

---

[10]During the fieldwork (January–March 2018), the exchange rate of one USD in the formal system was around 27.25 birr, while it was exchanged for around birr 33.50 in the black market. The difference of such amount of money is often considered too significant to ignore for the receiving families who are often poor.

that they would be intimidated by their lack of knowledge of how the system works[11].

Lack of access to banks in the receiving families' resident areas is another challenge identified as a factor that hinders the use of the formal money transfer system by the migrants (7.0 percent). In spite of the expansion of the banking network in Ethiopia in recent years, bank services are still inaccessible to the majority of the rural population. Many people from the rural areas need to travel to nearby towns to access the service.

The relatively high transaction cost and the slowness of the process to reach the money in time are the last two factors given by 5.0 per cent and 4.0 per cent of the former labour migrants, respectively, to use the formal remittance transfer system.

**The Informal Remittance Transfer Channels**

The second and most widely used system to send remittances back home is the informal remittance transfer channel. Unlike the formal system, informal transfer systems operate outside the conventional banking and financial channels and policies of the origin and/or the receiving countries[12]. Their operation is motivated by shared economic interest (of the senders, the receivers and the transfer agents) and characterized by swiftness, lower transaction costs, cultural convenience, reliability and easy accessibility.

Accordingly, Ethiopian migrants in the Republic of South Africa and the Middle East widely use the informal remittance transfer mechanisms. As indicated in Table 5 earlier, half of the migrants/returnees and 28 per cent of the families noted the use of the informal channels as a major means of transferring

---

[11]Focus group discussion in Halaba woreda with five returnees from the Middle East (February 22, 2018). Focus group discussion in Adigrat with eight returnees (five women and three men) (March 28, 2018).

[12]Although, as indicated earlier, the hawala system uses the formal banking system to dispatch the payment to the recipient within the country, the practice does not qualify as a formal system.

remittance. Actually, key informants identified two major types of informal systems. The first one is the transfer of money in person, and the second one is the use of the *hawala* institutions. According to key informants, transfer of money in person happens occasionally when one obtains the possibility of meeting someone travelling back to Ethiopia. On the positive side, it usually does not cost anything to transfer and the receiving person gets the cash in hard currency, which s/he can exchange at better rates in the black market in Ethiopia. However, on the negative side, in-person transfer of money is subject to high risk of losing the money as the person entrusted with the task may not always be trustworthy. All the risks associated with it are on the sender. As a result, migrants often take great precaution when they decide to send remittance in person.[13]

The second and widely used informal remittance channel is the *hawala* system. It is a system where someone in the migrant's country receives money in hard currency and his/her agent pays the recipient in local currency. The *hawala* system, according to the key informants, is highly preferred system of remittance transfer for three basic reasons. First, it provides 'much' better exchange rate than the formal channel[14]. Second, it is said to be very fast and efficient. It is indicated that families can receive their remittance money sent from the Republic of South Africa and the Middle East countries within two days at most. Third, it is very simple and does not require any documentation or

---

[13] Interview with Bedriya Mehdi, returnee migrant from Saudi Arabia (Halaba Special Woreda), Feb 26, 2018; Interview with Sadiya Ahmed, returnee migrant from Qatar, Shashemene, March 5, 2018; Interview with Hawi Samuel, Kofele *Woreda* Labour and Social Affairs Office. March 15, 2018.

[14] In September 2018 the exchange rate of one USD in banks is 27.50 *birr* while is exchanged for 32.50 *birr* in parallel informal market.

process either to send or receive.[15] The following story (Box 1) elucidates how migrants prefer the *hawala* system to the formal channel.[16]

**Box1:** Use of formal and informal remittance transfer from the view point of a migrant[17]

> My name is Alewiya. I lived in Saudi Arabia for about six years as a migrant worker. I was first employed in a big family as a maid through an Employment Agency with a two year contract. I worked in that family for one year and ten months. During this period, I used to send money to my family every three months through my employer. He was sending the money using Western Union and providing me the receipts. A very honest person! Just before my contract was over, I run away from there leaving my documents with my employer. I stayed with some friends for sometimes and began to work as an undocumented worker. The income was much better now. I asked my friends how I could send money to my family and they advised me to use *hawala*, which gives much better exchange rate and charges very little. I began to use the *hawala*. I simply give the money to my friend with the name and telephone number of the recipient and she passes the money and the information to the *hawala*. The next day, the agent of the *hawala* in Ethiopia calls my family with the number I gave and gives them the money either in cash or deposits it into their account in any bank. I used this system for the next four years I stayed in Saudi Arabia.

In fact, according to some experts in the bank and government offices, expansion of banking and mobile network in Ethiopia has led to the expansion and sophistication of the *hawala* system. Previously, the *hawala* dealer in Ethiopia used to call the recipient in a landline telephone number given by the

---

[15] Focus group discussion in Halaba Special *woreda* with five returnees from the Middle East (February 22, 2018). Focus group discussion in Adigrat with eight returnees from Saudi Arabia (five women and three men) (March 28, 2018), Interview with Yoseph Ayele, Shashemene, March 10, 2018.

[16] Interview with Alewiya Bedru, 28, a returnee migrant from Saudi Arabia, Shashemene, March 10, 2018.

[17] Interview with Ms. Alewiya Ahmed, a returnee from Saudi Arabia, Kofele, February 25, 2018.

sender. There was no way to ensure whether the person who picks the phone was the actual intended recipient or not. With that, the agent had additional task of ensuring the authenticity of the recipient before effecting the payment. Accordingly, the physical presence of the recipient with identity card was required to effect payments. With the expansion of the mobile telephone network, telephone numbers have become 'identity numbers'. Equally, the introduction and expansion of networked banking systems have greatly helped the transfer of money to the recipient families. The local agent of *hawala* operator would simply transfer the required sum of money in the bank account of the recipient. The task of ascertaining the authenticity of the identity of the recipient is, therefore, transferred to the banks. The narrative in Box 2 below shows how improvements in the telephone and banking system have contributed to the 'modernization' of the *hawala* system.

**Box 2:** Example of efficiency of informal remittance transfer[18]

> My sister is living in Dubai for the past 25 years. She sends money to support our elderly mother. She uses *hawala* all these times. Initially, I used to go to Addis Ababa to collect the money in cash. Later, with the introduction of mobile telephone and networked banking system, the agent of the *hawala* simply calls and asks me to give him my bank details. He would deposit the money in my account. It is very good as I do not bother to travel to Addis Ababa anymore and he does not bother to ensure my identity.

---

[18] Interview with Yoseph Ayele, Shashemene, March 11, 2018.

# 4 USE OF REMITTANCES AT HOUSEHOLD LEVEL

As observed from the results of the qualitative and quantitative data gathered for this study, there is a large inflow of remittance money in the study *woredas*. In the first place, the large proportion of the migrants, as indicated in Figure 6 below, decided to migrate with the objective of supporting their families. So, it is no wonder that most of the migrants send money back to their families in Ethiopia.

**Figure 6:** Reason for migration

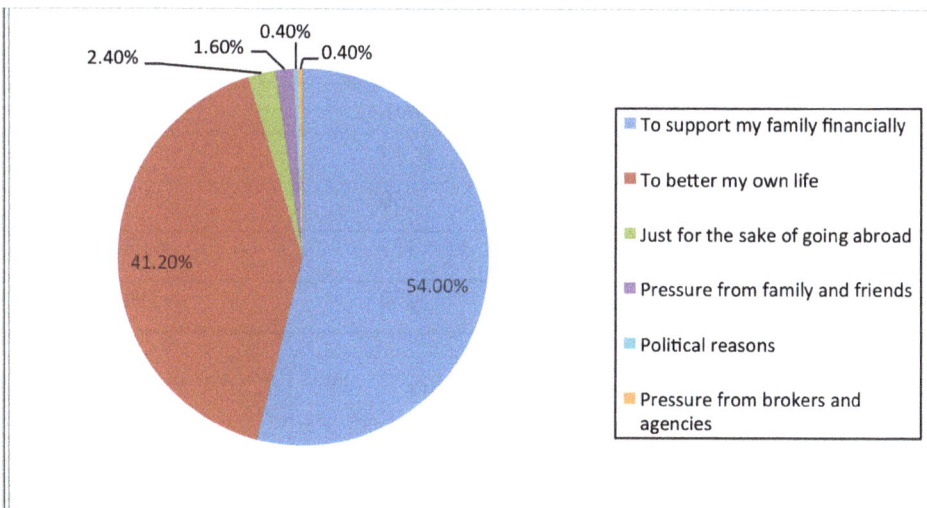

The fact that the majority of the migrants send money to their families was also shared by many of the key informant interviewees. For instance, Mr. Abebaw Wondimagegn, a key informant from Kombolcha, Amhara Region, said that a large number of households in his locality receive remittance money from their family members who work in Saudi Arabia or other Gulf States. As shown in Table 4 earlier, about 96 per cent of the returnee migrant respondents said that they used to send money to their families.

If almost all migrant workers send money to their families, it is, therefore, important to consider how the recipient families use the remittance money.

Families use remittance money in different ways depending of the size of the remittance money they receive and their economic conditions[19].In many cases, remittance money is primarily used to settle debt incurred by poor households to cover the cost of migration[20]. As shown in Table 7 below, 20 per cent of the returnee migrants from the Republic of South Africa and the Middle East said, they raised the money for their migration through loans and, hence, debt repayment is an important issue for many households[21]. In addition, remittance is used also to regain property such as land that was given as collateral when households secured loans to finance the migration of family members.

**Table 7**: Sources of money to finance migration of family members

| Source of money to finance migration | Responses | |
|---|---|---|
| | **Freq.** | **Percent** |
| Loans | 49 | 19.6 |
| My own savings | 30 | 12.0 |
| Family members' contribution | 171 | 68.4 |
| **Total** | **250** | **100** |

Next to repayment of debt, remittance money is used for a variety of reasons, including augmenting family resources to meet daily necessities, covering health and educational expenses, and purchasing household goods. As indicated in Table 8 below, 53.5 per cent of the remittance-receiving families used the remittance money mainly to cover household expenses, including food, children and sibling educational costs, clothing and healthcare[22].

---

[19] Interview with Yoseph Ayele, Shashemene, March 11, 2018.

[20] FDG with experts of Halaba Special *woreda* Women and Children's Affairs Office, Halaba, February 23, 2018

[21]In the finding of the survey for the returnees show that the migrants pay on average Birr 17,200 (USD 625.5) for the migration, while the response from the families show an average expense of birr 20,075 (730 USD).

[22] Interview with Mr. Tewodros Seifu, Overseas Employment Evaluation and Support Officer, Addis Ababa City Administration Bureau of Labour and Social Affairs. Date: 19/02/2018.

**Table 8:** Expenditure of remittance money by recipient families

| Purposes remittance money is used for | Responses | |
|---|---|---|
| | **Freq.** | **Percentage** |
| Household expenses such as health, schooling and clothing | 107 | 53.5 |
| To build a house | 30 | 15.0 |
| To purchase farm inputs such as fertilizer, seed, and oxen | 15 | 7.5 |
| To renovate a house | 14 | 7.0 |
| To buy furniture and other House Hold items | 9 | 4.5 |
| For saving | 7 | 3.5 |
| For renting in a house | 7 | 3.5 |
| To start a new business | 3 | 1.5 |
| For debt repayment | 3 | 1.5 |
| To buy a shop | 3 | 1.5 |
| For condominium payment | 2 | 1.0 |
| **Total** | **200** | **100** |

When we combine the data presented in Table 8, we learn that the majority of the families used the remittance money mainly for expenditure lines related to consumption. Here it is pertinent to ask why that was the case. This is due to two reasons. First, many of the migrant families are poor and hence they could not make a saving out of the remittance money they received (see Figure 6).[23] Second, as the migrant workers receive low salaries, the amount of remittance they could send to their families is small and, hence, it would not allow the majority of the households to make a saving for long-term investment and asset building (see Table 9 and the narrative in Box 3).

---

[23] Interview with Mohammed Ahmed, Education and Training Department Head, Kombolcha City Female, Children and Social Affairs Office, Kombolcha, Amhara Region. Date: 03/03/2018. And Interview with Sister Meria, Head, Tigray Regional Bureau of Social Affairs, Mekelle,

**Figure 7:** Percentage distribution of migrants' families by their sources of income

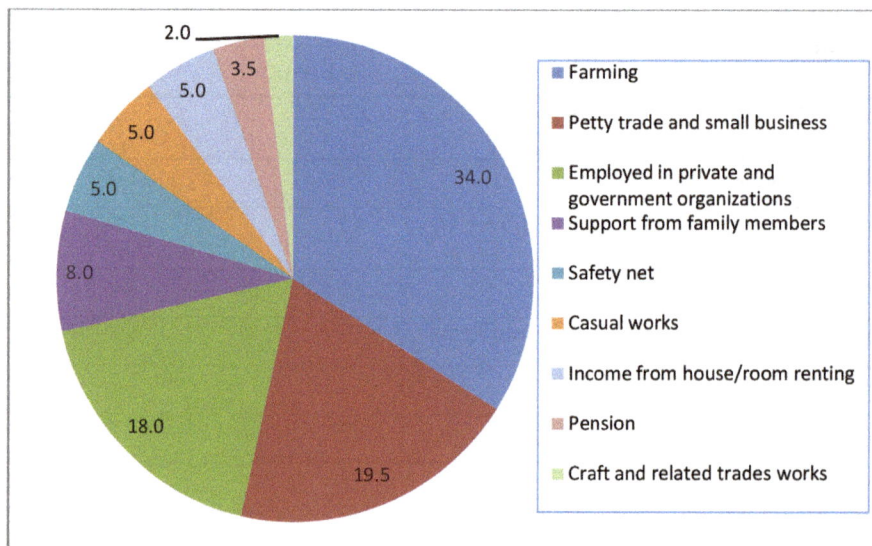

**Table 9**: Monthly income of migrants

| Amount of money(in Birr) | Percent |
|---|---|
| <1000 | 3.2 |
| 1,001–2,000 | 8.8 |
| 2,001–3,000 | 22.3 |
| 3,001–4,000 | 20.1 |
| 4,001–5,000 | 12.0 |
| 5,001–6,000 | 7.2 |
| 6,001–7,000 | 11.2 |
| 7,001–8,000 | 5.6 |
| 8,001–9,000 | 2.0 |
| 9001–10000 | 4.8 |
| >10001 | 2.8 |
| Total | 100.0 |

**Box 3:** Use of remittance money by households[24]

> I went to Saudi Arabia intending to change my family's life, mainly through asset building. At the end, however, I realized that it is impossible to do so. The problem is multifaceted. First, my payment/salary is too small. Thus, however hard one works, it is almost impossible to keep and store up life-changing money within a given period. From that little salary, one spends for oneself and to support family. With this, the money is gone. Secondly, the high inflation and cost of living in Ethiopia make saving and using the remittance money for asset building difficult. Even if one saves some money, say Birr 100,000, he or she can do little with it. Opening a kiosk needs more capital, let alone buying a house. People say, "in the good old times, by working for a few years in Saudi Arabia, they were able to make a big difference". This is now impossible. For that reason, many returnee migrants are frustrated and exposed to different kinds of illness, including mental problem.

The use of the remittance money for consumption, however, creates ill feelings among some migrant workers while they are abroad and after they returned. For instance, one FGD participant in Harbu said, "I used to earn 800 Saudi Riyals monthly and sent much of it to my family through the banks on three months frequency. However, when I came back home after three years, there was no change to the family –even the colour of our house was the same as I left it"[25].

As found out by this study, only close to 26 per cent of the migrants' families used the remittance money for asset building and saving. This means, almost three fourths of the families used the remittances largely for consumption. As a result, many migrant families have become dependent on remittance transfers. Indeed, there is a widely held feeling that families put pressure on migrant workers to continue working and keep on sending money. When the migrant workers return home after finishing their contract, they would face economic

---

[24] Interview with Bedriya Mehadi, a returnee migrant from Saudi Arabia, Halaba Special *woreda*, SNNPR, Date: Feb 26, 2018.

[25] FGD with Returnees in Kallu/Harbu, Date: 13/03/2018.

difficulties. In many cases, returnees could not even raise seed money required to get loan and other support from government employment schemes through Micro and Small Enterprises (MSEs) schemes. Reinforcing this argument, Walle Dagne, Dean of the Woreilu Technical and Vocational Education and Training College said that in the majority of the cases in his locality, many of the returnees could not even raise the 20 per cent capital required to secure loans from the Amhara Credit and Savings Institution (ACSI) which plays an important role in the region regarding job creation for the unemployed youth.[26]

Even if families of migrants used larger portions of remittances for consumption purposes, remittances help the revival of local economies and enable migrants' families to send children to school and to finance health care. (See, for example, the narratives in Boxes 4 and 5).

**Box 4:** Use of remittance money for supporting children's education[27]

> My two sisters are working as migrant workers in Saudi Arabia. Our parents are engaged in farming. Even if the income of the family was hand-to-mouth, it was sufficient to pay for basic expenses. The reason for the migration of my sisters was to improve their own livelihoods. The family covered the cost for the travel. Their monthly income is about 700 Saudi Riyal. The money they send is used to cover the expenses of their children.

**Box 5:** Use of remittance money for healthcare[28]

> Fifteen years ago, I decided to migrate to cover the medical cost of my mother. I divorced from my husband to travel to Saudi Arabia. I did not know how much money my family spent to cover the cost of my migration. It was my sister who, then working in Saudi Arabia, covered all the travel expenses. When I was working in Saudi Arabia, my monthly salary was 500 Saudi Riyals. I used to send all the money I was

---

[26] Interview with Walle Dagne, Dean, Woreilu TVET College. Woreilu, Date: 20/03/2018.
[27] FGD with Migrants Family Meeting place: Woreilu Meeting, Date: 20/03/2018.
[28] FGD with Returnees in Kallu/Harbu, Date: 11/03/2018.

> able to raise to my mother. The remittance money was used mainly to cover the medical cost of my mother who was ill at that time.

In addition to using remittance money to meet the costs of basic consumption, many households particularly, those in the urban areas, used remittance money to buy household goods —furniture and electronic goods such as television (TV) sets, satellite TV receivers and refrigerators. Moreover, households in Addis Ababa and other urban areas used the remittance money for the renovation of their houses.

While the majority of households, as discussed above, used remittance money for consumption, a small proportion of them were able to make savings and engage in asset building activities financed by remitted money. Indeed, close to 26 per cent of the migrant families reported their using remittance money for productive purposes in different forms. As shown in Table 8, the majority of the households are engaged in different kinds of asset building activities including: payment of government low cost (condominium) houses (1.5per cent), starting small businesses (1.4 per cent); purchasing shop (1.4per cent); purchasing oxen for farming and farm inputs (7.5per cent) and building houses (15.0per cent).From among those who say they make savings and engage in asset building activities, a small fraction of respondents (3.5%) said they make save in banks.

The use of remittance money for asset building has definitely positive implications on many households. To give few examples, households who entered into sharecropping arrangement due to lack of oxen were able to free themselves from such an arrangement by buying oxen using remittance money.[29] In some cases, as noted by Mrs. Yeshareg Tefera, Manager of ACSI) Woreilu Branch, families of migrant workers were able to transform their

[29] Interview with Abebaw Wondimagegn, Kombolcha, Amhara Region, Date: 16/03/2018.

farming system from subsistence to commercial farming by engaging in such activities as animal fattening[30].

When we look at the major means of asset building in the urban and rural areas, we see some differences. In the urban areas, the main means of asset building is the procurement of vehicles for doing business in the transport sector. The vehicles include three legged taxies (popularly known as *Bajaj*), small and minibus taxies. As noted by a key informant in Kirkos Sub-City of Addis Ababa, siblings who remain in the country were made to get trained in driving and served as drivers and then support the household with the money they make by providing transport services. In the rural areas, the most important and most common means of asset building using migrant remittances was the construction of houses[31]. In many cases, rental houses are built in nearby urban and peri-urban areas with the intention of generating sustainable income to the migrant households and creating asset for the reintegration of the migrant worker upon his/her return. There are, however, serious problems that threaten the use of this strategy for asset building. The first is the construction of houses in urban and peri-urban areas without securing house construction permits from municipalities, a fault which may be met by the demolition of houses and wastage of hard-earned savings, which were made by the migrant workers for many years[32]. Secondly, even if the use of remittances for construction of houses is a good strategy, as reported by key informants, in many cases, conflicts over ownership of property (houses) emerge when the migrant worker returns to his/her locality, as the house which was built using the remittance money is not registered in the name of the migrant worker[33]. This is not limited to houses; it also happens to other properties, such as vehicles. High prevalence

---

[30] Interview with Yeshareg Tefera, ACSI Woreilu Branch General Manager, Date: 20/03/2018.

[31] Interview with Mr. Alemu Maharo, returnee migrant from South Africa, Halaba Special *woreda*, SNNPR, Date: Feb 26, 2018; Interview with Jemal Seid, Dean, Kombolcha Agricultural College, Amhara Region, Date: 15 /03/2018.

[32] *Ibid.*

[33] Interview with Mr. Girma Tafete, Commercial Bank of Ethiopia, Woreilu Branch Customer Service Manager, 19.04.2018.

of familial disputes over money (savings) and asset procured using remittance money was reported in localities where there are a large number of migrants.[34] The narrative presented in Box 6 exemplifies those incidences.

**Box 6:** Familial dispute over remittance money[35]

> Jemila[36] worked for 20 years in Saudi Arabia. She was sending money to her uncle. She came two years ago when she fell very ill. When she approached her uncle for her money, he refused to give her the money, which he supposedly was safeguarding for her. She came to *the Woreda* Labour and Social Affairs Office and made her case. When her uncle was asked, he denied receiving the money she claimed. She went to court but finally dropped the case – because she could not stand in the court with her uncle. Later on, he only agreed to give her a small amount of the money she sent to him. He argued that whatever money she sent to him, he spent it on his children's education.

Even if the inflow of remittance money to families and communities is seen as positive way, remittance money could have also adverse repercussions on families and communities. First, according to informants, some families have become dependent on remittance transfers.[37]. Second, in some cases, as noted by informants, family members, largely husbands and young siblings (brothers) are accused of indulging in the use of addictive substances, such as *khat*, alcohol and tobacco (*shisha*) using the remittance money sent by the migrant workers.[38] Third, families of some migrants extravagantly spend the remittance money on unproductive investments such as purchase of ornaments, and celebration of religious festivals and other social events like weeding and memorials to the

---

[34] Interview with Mr. Birhane Mesfin, Kirkos Sub-city *woreda* 10 Labour and Social Affairs Office – Head, Date: 20/02/2018

[35] Interview: Biruk Yeshi, Social Worker – Addis Ketema Sub City *Woreda* 7 Labour and Social Affairs Office 13/02/2018.

[36] Original name is changed.

[37] Mohammed Ahmed, Department Head, Education and Training, Kombolcha City Women, Children and social Affairs Office, Kombolcha, Amhara Region. Date: 15/03/2018.

[38] Mohammed Ahmed, Education and Training Department Head, Kombolcha City Women, Children and Social Affairs Office, Kombolcha, Amhara Region. Date: 15/07/2018.

dead.[39]Although such activities have important social functions, the of migrant families' tendency to spend more than families that do not receive remittance, according to our informants, weakens the possibility of using remittances for saving and asset building activities.[40] Box 7 presents a narration of such a case in point.

**Box 7:** Recipient families' expenditure of remittance money[41]

> Kalu *woreda* is highly affected by the migration of young people to the Arab countries. In the past few years, a large number of young people including civil servants and graduates of higher learning institutions have migrated to work in the Gulf countries. Without exaggeration, almost every household has at least one member of it serving as a migrant worker abroad; and most migrants remit money to their family back home. Due to the inflow of remittance money to the locality, living styles of the local people have been changing. Some families also engaged in extravagant and unproductive expenditure of the remittance money. In some cases, households organize a traditional prayer ceremony called '*wodaja*', which require expenditure of a large sum of money. For this ceremony, a large number of people including relatives and friends are served food and drinks. The way families spend remittance money has negative repercussion on migrant workers. When the migrant workers return home, they will learn that the families have spent all the money they sent them back. They could not find any support for their reintegration. They have two choices – one is migrating again, the other is re-entering the poverty they tried to escape by migrating.

Even if there is a realization among local officials that a large amount of money comes to their localities through remittance, according to informants, no concerted effort was made by local governments and non-governmental organizations to encourage remittance recipients to use the remittance money (at

---

[39] Interview with Jemal Seid, Harbu *Kebele* Job Creation, Education and Training Expert, Kalu *woreda*, Kombolcha, Date 14/03/2018.

[40]*Ibid.*

[41]*Ibid.*

least some portion of it) for saving and asset building.[42] Instead, the government and donors have developed programmes which aim at the rehabilitation of returnees from the Gulf countries.[43]

---

[42] *Ibid.*

[43] *Ibid.*

# 5    CONCLUSION AND RECOMMENDATIONS

The magnitude of international migration from Ethiopia has substantially increased in recent decades owing to various political, social and economic factors. Since the 1990s, the Republic of South Africa and oil-rich Middle East countries have emerged as major destinations of the significant portion of Ethiopian labour migrants. Labour migration to the Middle East contains both documented and undocumented migrants; and most of the migrants to the Republic of South Africa did not secure the required permits.

The Ethiopian diaspora and migrant workers remit a large sum of money to the country for a variety of reasons, ranging from assisting their families to investment. Indeed, in recent years, remittance flows to Ethiopia have become important sources of foreign currency. In this regard, the National Bank of Ethiopia (NBE) reported that the amount of remittance flowing to Ethiopia has increased from 3.04 billion USD in 2013/14 to 3.99 billion USD in 2015/16 (NBE 2016).There is a limited understanding about those factors that influence the choice of migrants between using formal and informal channels of remittance transfer and how remittances influence the socio-economic wellbeing of households. Based on these premises, this research report examined the various channels through which Ethiopian labour migrants in the Republic of South Africa and the Middle East send remittances to their families; and how remittances are utilized at household levels.

The quantitative data and qualitative information for the study were collected from ten systematically selected *woredas*, two from each of the Tigray, Amhara, Oromia and SNNP regions and Addis Ababa City Administration. These *woredas* were selected based on the prevalence of migration to the Republic of South Africa and the Middle East, the flow of remittances, and the presumed socio-economic impacts. Different methods of data collection were applied to gather the necessary primary and secondary data. Two surveys were undertaken: one for the returnee migrants and the other for families of migrants. In addition, the research team conducted key informant interviews and focus group discussions. The primary data were augmented by secondary data.

The major findings of the study are summarised as follows. First, almost all of the returnees 97 per cent) used to send money to their families back home. Also 92 per cent of families of migrants acknowledged their receiving remittances through different channels. The widespread practice of sending remittances by migrant workers could be explained by the primary motive for their migration – desire to improve their and their families' livelihood.

Second, remittances are sent using the formal and informal channels and sometimes using both. The formal and the informal channels have their own respective advantages and drawbacks. About 50 per cent of returnees reported that banks and money transfer institutions (such as Western Union and Money Gram) were their preferred channels, while the remaining 50per cent said they were using individuals travelling to the country and informal *hawala.* Whereas, the majority (72 per cent) of families of the migrants claim that they receive remittance through banks and money transfer institutions, while only 28 per cent asserted they received remittances through informal channels. The reported high proportion of families receiving remittance money through banks does not explain the growth of the formal transfer system. It instead shows the growing use of the banks by the informal operators. This is due to the expansion of commercial banks and the mobile network.

Third, the formal transfer systems, according to returnee migrants, are reliable and the chance of losing one's money is almost nil. The money transferred through the formal system contributes to the national economy by bringing foreign currency to the banking system. In spite of its reliability and contribution to the national economy, however, the use of the formal transfer system is hampered by some serious limitations. Those limitations include the requirement by money transfer institutions for migrants to present valid passport and residence permits in the host country; lower exchange rates in comparison to the informal market; the difficulty migrants face to use the formal system in

the host countries because of language problems; and the high cost of financial transfer.

On the other hand, the informal system of transferring money is trust based and operates traditionally outside the conventional banking and financial channels and is motivated by shared economic interests of the sender, the receiver and the transfer agent. Advantages from the informal system include lower transfer cost, and speedy transfer and easy accessibility of the remittance. The expansion of core banking systems and mobile phones has greatly helped the transfer of money to the recipient families through the informal system. This means the expansion of banks does not necessarily correlate with the increment of formal remittance transfers. Indeed, informal money transfer agents who collect hard currencies abroad use the banks to deliver the remittance money to the recipient families. This shows the interface (interconnection) that prevails between the formal and the informal systems of transferring money.

The study also examined the use of remittance money at the household level. The money is used for different purposes, including debt resettlement, consumption and pursuing asset-building endeavours. Much of the remittance money is, however, used for consumption, such as paying for basic necessities, education and healthcare.

A small number of recipient families use the remittance money for (productive) asset-building purposes. There is a slight variation in how asset-building activities are carried out in the rural and urban setting. In the rural areas, the main means of asset building has been construction of houses in newly emerging towns and nearby peri-urban and urban areas. Those houses which are built in urban centres could be rented out to fetch some income to the families. In the urban areas, families use the remittance money to start small businesses. In many cases, migrant families purchase vehicles to start transport services.

Even if the inflow of remittances has certainly positive implications for families and communities, the manner in which it is used could have also adverse repercussions. The fact that migrant families use large portions of the remittance money for consumption could make them to be increasingly dependent on remittances. This is largely because of the small size of remittances and the poor economic conditions of the recipient families. Furthermore, the use of remittances predominantly for consumption contradicts young people's aspiration to improve their lives by working, and even through migration.

The findings of the study lend for key recommendations, which can be directed categorically to the different actors:

## I. Recommendations for the Government of Ethiopia (GoE)

The GoE should:

- Devise an overall migration policy that directs its actions in a harmonised manner. Such a policy is important considering the youthfulness of the country's population. A migration policy should envision the development of skilled human resource, which could compete in the international labour market.

- Promote safe and regular labour migration. Ensuring better pay, safe working conditions and protection for those who migrate following the formal (legal) channel of migration has many advantages. Among others, it reduces the number of people who decide to migrate without securing the required permits by both the Ethiopian and host governments. Migrants who have the required documentations would not face problems with regard to access to financial services; and hence, documented migration encourages use of the formal transfer of remittance to Ethiopia.

- Enter into Bilateral Labour Agreements (BLA) with Middle Eastern and others countries, which have a need for expatriate labour force. Such agreements are important instruments not only to enhance documented and safe migration but also to help in providing protection to migrant workers.

- Provide migrants with pre-departure training on financial literacy. Such training could encourage migrant workers to develop visions and to have awareness about opening bank accounts, saving and remittance transfer systems.

- Devise, at the levels of regional and local administrations, ways that would ensure the construction of houses by remittance-receiving families meet the required legal formalities. One way to encourage asset building through construction of houses is supporting the establishment of housing cooperatives by migrant workers and their families.

- Orient, empower and support, at the levels of regional and local administrations, remittance-recipient families and returnee migrants on the use of remittances for productive purposes (creation of employment through micro- and small- enterprises) by providing skills training and loans.

- Devise well thought out financial policies and mechanisms in order to narrow down the gaps between the official and unofficial rates of currency exchange.

- Expand the accessibility of formal financial institutions throughout the country.

## II. Recommendations for the Governments of the Migrant-Hosting Countries

The governments of the migrant-hosting countries should do the following:

- Promote safe and documented migration and find ways and means to regularize irregular migrant workers. Such a measure helps to reduce the vulnerability of the migrant workers and reduce irregular/informal employment.

- Provide protection to migrant workers by incorporating international norms (conventions) which provide guidelines for the protection of the rights of migrant workers.

- Devise ways that will promote transfer of remittances through the formal channel. One way to do this is to collaborate with the Government of

Ethiopia and/or its consular offices on the issuance of valid identity documents (like passport) that could be acceptable to the financial institutions.

## II. Recommendations for Financial Institutions

- Ethiopian banks and financial institutions should expand the accessibility of the money transfer agencies to the migrant workers;

- Ethiopian banks and financial institutions should lower fees on transferring remittances via the formal channels;

- In addition to the already existing incentives, Ethiopian banks should provide financial products and incentives that could motivate migrant workers to transfer their remittances through the formal system. One way to do this is to provide privileges, such as higher interest rates to members of the diaspora if they open a saving account and transfer their savings in hard currencies.

## V. Recommendations for International Agencies and Civil Society Organizations

International Agencies and Civil Society Organizations should:

- Advocate and promote safe and documented labour migration and strive for the regularisation of undocumented migrant workers;

- Advocate for the protection of the rights of migrant workers both in the host and origin countries;

- Promote financial literacy with migrant workers both before and after their departure; and

- Support migrant workers and their families in using remittances for pursuing asset-building activities.

# REFERENCES

Adams Jr, R. H.
  2011 Evaluating the economic impact of international remittances on developing countries using household surveys: A literature review. *Journal of Development Studies,* 47(6):809–828.

Adams Jr. R.H. and J. Page
  2005 Do international migration and remittances reduce poverty in developing countries? *World Development,* 33(10):1645–1669.

Alemayehu G., T. Kibrom, and A. Meleket
  2011 Remittance and remittance service providers in Ethiopia. *IAES Working Paper Series,* NO. A02/2011.

Alemayehu G. and J. Irving
  2011 Remittance and remittance service providers in Ethiopia. ***In*** Mohapatra, S. and D. Ratha (Eds.), *Remittance Markets in Africa,* 113–132. The World Bank, Washington DC.

Anderson, Lisa
  2014 Migration, remittances and household welfare in Ethiopia. *UNU-Merit Working Paper Series.* United Nations University.

Asnake Kefale and Zerihun Mohammed
  2015 Ethiopian labour migration to the Gulf and South Africa. *FSS Monograph,* No.10. Forum for Social Studies, Addis Ababa.

De Haas, H.
  2007 Remittances, Migration and Social Development: A Conceptual Review of the Literature. Social Policy and Development Programme Paper No. 34, United Nations Research Institute for Social Development

Demissie, F.
  2017 "Ethiopian female domestic workers in the Middle East and Gulf States: An introduction". *African and Black Diaspora: An International Journal.* 11(1).

Fernandez, Bina.
  2009. Disposable in the Downturn? Ethiopian Domestic Workers in the Gulf. University of Leeds.

Gebre, L.T., P. Maharaj and N.K. Pillay

2011 "The experiences of immigrants in South Africa: A case study of Ethiopians in Durban, South Africa". *Urban Forum*, 22(1).

Bina, H.

2010 "Cheap and disposable? The impact of the global economic crisis on the migration of Ethiopian women domestic workers to the Gulf." *Gender and Development*, 18(2):249–62.

Forum for Social Studies (FSS)

2017 Socio-economic assessment migration and labour market: 'Stemming irregular migration in Northern and Central Ethiopia (SINCE)'. Report for International Labour Organization (ILO). Unpublished. Forum for Social Studies. http://www.ilo.org/wcmsp5/groups/public/---africa/---ro-addis_ababa/---sro-addis_ababa/documents/publication/wcms_613907.pdf accessed on July 15, 2018.

Ghosal, S.

2015 Workers' remittances, one of the reliable sources of capital inflows to Ethiopia – Its performance analysis towards shaping the economic growth. *International Journal of Interdisciplinary and Multidisciplinary Studies,* 2(6):174–185.

Isaacs, L.

2017 Research study to enhance the volume and value of formal remittances to Ethiopia. ACP-EU Migration Action. International Organization for Migration, Brussels, Belgium.

Kapur, D.

2003 Remittances: The New Development Mantra? Paper prepared for the G-24 Technical Group Meeting.

Ratha, Dilip

2003 Worker's Remittances: An Important and Stable Source of External Development Finance. In Global Development Finance: Striving for Stability in Development Finance (157–75). Washington DC: The World Bank

Mohapatra, S. and D. Ratha

2011. "Migrant remittances in Africa: An overview," *In* Mohapatra, S. and D. Ratha (Eds.), *Remittance markets in Africa.* World Bank, Washington, D.C.

National Bank of Ethiopia (NBE)

2016 Annual Report, 2015/16. Addis Ababa: NBE.

Nisah, Christian and F. Bichaka

2018 "Remittances to Africa and Economics" *In* Monga, C. and J.Y. Lin (Eds.),*The Oxford Handbook of Africa and Economics*. Oxford, Oxford University Press.

Ratha, D.

2003 Worker's remittances: An important and stable source of external development finance. *In Global Development Finance: Striving for Stability in Development Finance* (157–75). The World Bank, Washington, D.C.

Sander, C. and S. M. Maimbo

2005 Migrant remittances in Africa: A regional perspective. *In* Maimbo, S. M. and D. Ratha (Eds.), *Remittances: Development Impact and Future Prospects* (53–79). The World Bank, Washington D, C.

Taylor, J.E.

1999 The New Economics of Labour Migration and the role of remittances in the migration process. *International Migration,* 37(1): 63–88.

United Nations

2017 *International Migration Report 2017: Highlights.* Department of Economic and Social Affairs, United Nations, New York.. ST/ESA/SER.A/404.

United Nations Conference on Trade and Development (UNCTAD)

2012. *The Least Developed Countries Report, 2012*. UNCTAD, Geneva.

World Bank

2016*Remittance and Migration Factbook.* 3$^{rd}$ edition. The World Bank, Washington DC.

World Bank

2017 Migration and remittances: Recent developments and outlook. Special topic: Global compact on migration. *Migration and Development*

*Brief*, 27 April 2017. The World Bank and the Global Knowledge Partnership on Migration and Development (KNOMAD).

World Bank.

2011 Migration and Remittances Factbook 2011.Washington, DC: World Bank.

Yang, D.

2011 "Migrant remittances", *Journal of Economic Perspectives*, 25( 3)

www.ingramcontent.com/pod-product-compliance
Lightning Source LLC
Chambersburg PA
CBHW080555270326
41929CB00019B/3327